Seeking God
For Your
Financial Bailout

By

Wendy Evans

Innovo™
Publishing

Seeking God for Your Financial Bailout

Published by
Innovo Publishing, LLC.

Copyright © 2009 by Wendy Evans
All rights reserved.

ISBN 13: 978-0-9815403-4-4
ISBN 10: 0-9815403-4-1

Cover Design & Interior Layout: Innovo Publishing, LLC

Printed in the United States of America
U.S. Printing History

First Edition: March 2009

Dedication

This book is dedicated to God, Jesus and the Holy Spirit for all that they have poured into me, enabling me to rise up to the challenge of writing this book after one of the darkest periods of my life. In December 2008, I had just gotten out of the hospital and the same day found a message on my cell phone from the president of my workplace. I called back only to find out that I had been laid off from my job of five and a half years.

The next day, I had to rush my dad to the hospital in an ambulance. It was discovered that he had pneumonia and had had it for months, but it had gone completely undiagnosed by his normal doctor. The doctors had already decided that my dad was dying and that he had cancer. After much prayer, God intervened. Today my dad is still alive and he is doing well. All glory to God!

One day later, my boyfriend's truck was hit in an accident, luckily while unoccupied.

A few days later I got a call that my aunt was in the hospital suffering from complications from a previous surgery.

The travail was unbearable; too much in too short a period of time. On top of this, I was in a constant fight with my noisy next-door neighbors.

The trials continued; I was promised another job by my previous employer only to find that someone who had been with the company less than a year was given the job. I was never even given a chance to interview for the position. My previous employer called to set up another interview. I accepted but then he cancelled my appointment a couple hours before I was due to be there. This same employer later contacted me and asked me if I'd be interested in a temporary job in the same department to replace someone who was taking pregnancy leave. The understanding was that as soon as the pregnant employee decided to return to work, I would be laid off again. I said no.

God began to help me deal with the tribulations I had been through, and He began to stir my spirit with a new message that he wanted to get out to the world to bring about change. With so many problems, broken promises, and disappointments in my life, I climbed into God's presence and let Him pour into me.

I pray that this book brings God glory and helps everyone who reads it to find greater knowledge of who God is and what He is trying to do in their lives. The cost of the oil in my alabaster box has been great, so enjoy the book, make the changes that God is requiring, and watch God change things around!

Acknowledgments

I would like to thank the following people for supporting me, listening to my wild ideas and my great hopes, and comforting me through much tribulation: Michael Schmidt, my beloved fiancé; Lenoard and Rosie Crear, my parents; Rev. Billy Crear, my brother; Cynthia Crear and Sharon Bryant, my sisters.

Additional thanks to Barbara Mack and Glynn Hagins for supporting me in the ministry and for always praying for me and being a source of inspiration.

Thanks to ICCM ministry for being a beacon of light to me and helping me to find my way.

I'd like to thank Mike Murdock for stirring my heart towards the ministry, and I'd like to thank Bishop TD Jakes because he has been a beacon of light, a mentor, a friend, and a brother to me. I'd also like to thank Bishop TD Jakes for the impartation of the knowledge that he has shared with me, and for the opportunities that he has given me to work with him in a ministry setting.

Thanks to Bart of Innovo Publishing for all of his help, and special thanks to all of my friends that supported me during this time of transition, especially Elijah Weaver.

Additionally, I'd like to thank Thelma Wells and Bishop Eddie Long for making the Word of God come alive in my life.

And most of all I thank God for all of you because you are His gift to me to help propel me up the steps of the destiny that he ordained for me before my conception in the womb!

Table of Contents

Chapter 1

Seeking God For Your Financial Bailout

As incredible as it is, God has allowed this country to have its first black president, Barack Obama. It is an unrealistic expectation to place on an individual to think that this country's finances will change overnight just because Barack Obama is president. To place such an expectation on one person will undoubtedly lead to disappointment, frustration, and a broken cistern. God allows leaders to be raised up to assist Him in accomplishing His purpose. Therefore, the leader that God has allowed to be raised up is not the ultimate and final decision maker in any matter, God is. Leaders do not really have the final say in finances, economic readjustments, health reforms, tax reforms, etc. Psalm 24:1 states that the earth is the Lord's and the fullness thereof. God is sovereign and has sovereign authority over all of the earth and ultimately everyone and everything in it. Therefore, if you need a financial bailout, petitioning God for your financial bailout is your answer—not your employer, and not the government.

There is no doubt that because Barack Obama was elected, God will undoubtedly be able to do amazing things through the new president and his chosen administration. However, God does not want you to have an inappropriate view of who holds all of the power in the world. The current economic state of the world exists because of a multitude of reasons. To place blame and to point fingers will change nothing and accomplish nothing. God has allowed this country to be in its current state because He wants the world's attention. When everything is going well, the world has no need for God, prayers are few and far between, and people are not really interested in a relationship with God or the church. When things are bad, people hurt, they want comfort, and they then cry out to God for help. Donations at most churches are way down, people are getting laid off because of the economy. Food prices are rising, fuel costs are slowly rising, electrical costs are rising—all costs are rising, but incomes are not keeping up, and there is not enough money to meet our current needs.

God wants the world's attention because the world needs to change! God poured into my spirit some of what He sees that needs changing:

1. Some Church leaders have become corrupt. Church leaders have lost their focus. Church leaders have lost their passion for the ministry and for the people that God sends. The original call that God placed on ministers' lives has been replaced by the ministry operating as a business for profit with little or no concern for the people that God has given them to shepherd. Churches are more interested in driving the dollars in and how many people show up to services than they are about winning souls to Christ and helping God grow His kingdom.

2. Parents, businessmen/women, CEO's, executives, hourly and salaried employees have become desensitized to life and to their children, their families and their friends. They have given up their life in exchange for a job. People that work in companies give their best to the people they work with, but treat their family members, their spouses, and their extended family members with cold disdain. People in this state are mentally, physically and emotionally unavailable to

their family, their children, and their friends.

3. Heads of corporations are more interested in discarding people who have served them faithfully for years than they are in making less profits and empowering the people that have served them to live secure financial and well-balanced lives.

4. Politicians are more interested in telling people whatever is necessary to get themselves reelected than they are in making the proposed changes and revisions that got them elected in the first place.

5. The government is more interested in excessively overtaxing people and inflicting pain upon them because they cannot pay the excessive fines and fees they charge than they are in offering a forgiveness program that wipes the slate clean and gives people a new start.

6. Certain retailers overprice their merchandise and have sales, such as black Friday, that create competition, fights and even stampedes that can result in serious injuries or even death. Retailers are drastically increasing their prices on food, clothes, shoes, and household items for the sake of profits, and they are causing many to go hungry because they cannot afford the increased costs.

7. The elderly are discarded, made fun of, locked up in nursing homes and kept doped up. The elderly are denied benefits, rights and opportunities because they are old. The elderly are not treated with the respect or dignity they deserve.

8. Criminals commit hate crimes against others, and it is often excused as acceptable behavior, or there is insufficient evidence to convict them.

9. The guilty go free and the innocent suffer or pay the long-suffering price for the guilty.

10. People are having sex before marriage and calling it "choice".

11. Married people are having sex with others and calling it "an alternative lifestyle".

12. Drug dealers are selling drugs and calling it "escaping to a new reality".

13. Same sex couples are having sex with each other and calling it "liberation".

14. Insurance companies are defrauding consumers and customers and refusing to pay valid claims and calling it "smart business practices".

15. Hospitals are understaffed, forcing patients admitted to have to care for themselves or have someone else care for them and calling it "budget revisions".

16. Schools are downsizing and overworking employees and calling it "reduction in forces".

17. Providers of services overcharge on their prices, then do not deliver what was promised and call it "a fluke in the system".

18. The homeless, the children, the widows, and the single mothers are forced to make ends meet on barely nothing, and it is called "apply for welfare".

The list could go on and on, but these are examples of injustices in the world that prevent a Holy God from restoring the world to be a better place. If you are a victim of today's economic downfall, I encourage you to examine yourself, examine your motives and determine if you fit into any of the clearly defined categories of injustices that are currently going on in the world. If you see yourself in any of the aforementioned categories, or if you know that you are not the type of person you should be, then it is time for you to change and repent. For each person that changes and repents, the world becomes a better place because of your true repentance and true change. The world then becomes a step closer to being a better place to live.

If after reading the aforementioned list you see yourself in one of the categories, your first step is to repent before God. To repent means to turn from the direction in which your life is currently going and change your ways. You must humble yourself before God and ask for His forgiveness for your previous and current behavior in whatever situation you may find yourself. As human beings, you may find it impossible to change yourself, and this is why God offers to help you when you submit yourself to Him humbly and invite Him into your life to help you change. If you do not see yourself in any of the aforementioned categories, but you know you are guilty of not giving God your very best or not being in the right relationship with the people God has placed in your life, you need to repent. The following prayer will help you open up a prayer dialogue with God whereby you can quickly and easily start your process towards repentance:

> Holy God, creator of Heaven and Earth, please forgive me for my previous wrong ways of thinking, forgive me for my wrong ways of behaving, the previous ways that I've treated people, and for the poor choices that I've made concerning my life. Come into my heart and come into my life to cleanse from me all unrighteousness and lead me back into a right relationship and a right fellowship with You. Create in me a pure heart, Oh God, and renew in me a steadfast spirit, Psalm 51:10. Remember not the sins of my youth, and my rebellious ways; according to your love remember me, for you are good, Oh Lord, Psalms 25:7. Have mercy upon me, Oh God, according to your unfailing love, according to your great compassion blot out my transgression, Psalm 51:1. Dear God, demonstrate your unfailing love for me by forgiving me and by being tender to me and helping me to change and walk worthy in your sight, so

that I can receive from your hand the financial bailout plan that you have for me. In Jesus' mighty matchless name I ask and pray. Amen.

Chapter 2

Expediting Your Financial Bailout From God

God responds to those who enter into His presence in a variety of ways. God will most often respond to you and your request of Him when you are:

1. Obedient to Him or His word.
2. When you are following His directions.
3. When you are broken and humbled before Him.

Undoubtedly you have already prayed, undoubtedly you may already feel bad about your current situation and/or circumstances, and undoubtedly you have already tried to get out of your current situation yourself. You need God's power and intervention to get out of your current circumstances, God only supplies the power necessary to get you out of your situation when you have either been obedient to Him, humbled yourself before Him, or when you are following His directions. God intervenes as the need arises for him to do so. God intervenes when plans need to be altered, changed or diverted to remain in line with his sovereign plans and or purposes for your life. So when you cooperate with God's redemptive purposes for allowing you to be in your current state of being, and when you make the changes that God is requiring you to make, then receiving your financial bailout from God will become easier and quicker.

To expedite the process of entering into God's presence, begin a fast whereby you abstain from food for eight days. Since you may not be used to fasting, it is highly recommended that you do just a mini fast for eight days. A fast unto the Lord is a special time that you set aside to pray to and hear from the Lord concerning your specific situation.

Fasting clears your mind, humbles you, and makes you more in tune with God's spirit. God will speak more clearly into your life, and He will show you what is wrong and what you need to do to repair it. When you hear from God and He shows you what you need to do to repair what is wrong, you will then be well on your way to receiving your financial bailout from God. During your fast you should decide the following:

1.   Determine what your fast will consist of. Juice, tea, water and coffee are recommended during your fast – food is not recommended.

2.   Commit to a time allotment of how long you will fast daily. Set a time allotment that you can commit to, an hour, two hours, etc.

3.   Commit to fasting for at least eight days. The number eight denotes resurrection, new beginnings, regeneration, new birth. You need God to give new birth to your finances and a new beginning to your life.

God said in 2 Chronicles 7:14: "If my people who are called by name will humble themselves and pray and seek my face and turn from their wicked ways, then will I hear from Heaven and will forgive their sin and heal their land."

Biblical fasting is abstaining from eating food for the sole purpose of communicating directly with God. Fasting within itself has no power, the fact that you are consecrating yourself unto God to seek His face regarding your situation and/or circumstances is what will draw God's power to you. When you consecrate yourself, you are setting yourself apart from your normal activities or functions for the sole purpose of connecting with a most high and Holy God. Although you may not receive your financial bailout from God overnight, God will respond to you, and He will begin to work on your situation to bring about healing and restoration when you make the changes or lifestyle modifications He is calling you to make.

Types of fasts suggested

1. Regular fast – No food and no liquids.
2. Partial fast – Only liquids such as coffee, water, tea, or juice. No food.

Length of time for your fast suggested

It is suggested that you fast for a minimum of two hours a day for eight days. If you fast only for one hour, you may be so busy telling God how you feel and what you want that you do not leave any room for Him to tell you how He feels and what He wants. God will often speak back to you in a still, small voice. If you have trouble discerning how God speaks to you, it is highly recommended that you speak with your pastor of your local church for help and guidance on how to discern God's voice. Your pastor may be able to refer you to classes, or to give you resources on how best to proceed.

- What should you do during your fast?
- You should pray, pray, and then pray, and then listen, listen and then listen.

Prayer to get you started during your fast

Lord, God, send revival, send revival of my finances, my life, my health and all that pertains to me. Breathe new life into the dead places in my life as Jesus brought Lazarus back to life after death, John 11:44. Dear God, please bring additional funding sources and additional help to revive and restore me to the right financial standing. If I have erred in the budgeting of my money, send me help, guidance and assistance so that I may learn and come to an understanding of how you want and expect me to manage my money. God, rescue me from this miry pit of despair, rescue me from a corruptible end, intervene and save me as only You can. Change the current financial afflictions I am facing. Change the current economic crises the world is facing. Dear God, since You have knowledge on what caused this downfall in the economic situation, change rulers in high places who lead and make decisions that are not in the economy's best interests. Change rulers that do not honor You or Your value system for Your people. Change rules that do not honor or value Your Holy statues and Your way of doing things; replace these rulers with God-fearing men and or women who love, honor and serve You and that will make good and Godly decisions for the world and for the betterment of the economy. Unseat those rulers in high places whose morals, judgments and values do not line up with Your plans, Your preferred expectations or Your purposes. Most Holy God, have mercy upon me, but I pray that You deal with those leaders who are causing division, distortion, layoffs, early terminations, and death. I pray that you will convict the guilty and let the innocent go free. In Jesus' mighty name I pray. Amen.

Notice that God's promises are often conditional. Deuteronomy 11:26-28 gives a clear example of God's view on His blessings: "See, I am setting before you today a blessing and a curse – the blessing if you obey the commands of the LORD your God that I am giving you today; the curse if you disobey the commands of the LORD your God and turn from the way that I command you today by following other gods, which you have not known." If you want to be able to receive God's promises, you have got to meet

God's terms and/or conditions. In addition, carefully study Bible scriptures on God's promises for financial prosperity. By studying the scriptures your faith and expectation will begin to rise and grow as you dig deeper into God's Word.

The following examples are great promises to claim regarding God's promise to help you prosper:

- Deuteronomy 28:11: "The LORD will grant you abundant prosperity – in the fruit of your womb, the young of your livestock and the crops of your ground – in the land he swore to your forefathers to give you."
- Job 22:21: "Submit to God and be at peace with him; in this way prosperity will come to you."
- Job 36:11: "If they obey and serve him, they will spend the rest of their days in prosperity and their years in contentment."
- Psalm 25:13: "He will spend his days in prosperity, and his descendants will inherit the land."
- Proverbs 3:2: "For they will prolong your life many years and bring you prosperity."
- Proverbs 8:18: "With me are riches and honor, enduring wealth and prosperity."
- Proverbs 13:21: "Misfortune pursues the sinner, but prosperity is the reward of the righteous."
- Isaiah 45:7 " I form the light and create darkness, I bring prosperity and create disaster; I, the LORD, do all these things."

Your current financial situation did not occur overnight. Even if you are just experiencing the results of your financial downfall, often the problem began long before the problem actually surfaced in your life and became a issue. When you follow the steps given in this book, it will be up to God how quickly you get out of your current financial circumstances. You may be more interested in just simply getting out of your situation, God is, however, more interested in you changing and becoming more Christ-like, so you will finally be able to experience peace and happiness. In addition, He can work through you to reach others who could be in a similar or worse situation. If your life is in a financial mess, it is like that for a reason. If you are not generating enough income in your life, it is like that for a reason. Only God knows the reason it is like that, to find out the answer to that question, you have to ask God.

Pain is usually the only way that God can get someone's attention. If you want your pain to stop, get right with God. Make the changes necessary to become a better person. Repent before God, fast before God for two hours each day, pray daily, and do whatever it is that God tells you to get your financial bailout from God. If you repent and your heart is really changed, give God eight days and see what He will do with your life, your finances, your mind, your marriage, your family, your hopes and your dreams. As you draw closer to God during your times of fasting, surrender all of your "baggage" to Him, surrender all of your "fears" to Him and let Him decide how best to work out your problems. If you could have fixed your own problems, they would already be fixed, you need God's power to intervene and bring about the lasting changes that your life needs and desires.

As you have probably noticed, what you are currently doing is not working, what do you have to lose by giving God an eight-day fast? The key to this self-introspection process is not to determine how and who you think you are with God, but to discover who God thinks you are before Him. God created you, and He holds the blueprints for your original design, only He knows if your current character, your current integrity, your current desires, and your current lifestyle fits the blueprint that He designed for your life.

In today's society, wearing an accepted mask has become the accepted norm. No one is what they seem. People pretend to be someone or something they are not for material gain, spiritual gain, and for financial gain. Being transparent before God and admitting who you are before God when you take your mask off is a vital step towards much-needed change.

Ask yourself the following questions:

1. Who are you when you take your mask off?
2. Why do you behave the way you currently do? (To fit in, are you forced into being that way?)
3. What are your feelings about how you treat your spouse, your family, your kids, and your friends?
4. Are you physically and emotionally present in your current relationships? (If not, where is your mind, and why are you not present in the moment that God has given you?)
5. Are you kind to the people around you? Why or why not?
6. Do you inflict pain on others? Verbally, mentally or emotionally? Why is it necessary for you to inflict so much pain on others?
7. Do you have unresolved issues that are causing you to behave the way that you currently are?
8. Have you considered getting professional help? (A counselor, social worker, or a psychologist?) Why or why not?

Chapter 3

What Does God Want?

God wants each and every person He created to have a growing relationship with Him and a growing knowledge of who He is and why He created you. God wants each and every person that He created to accept His one and only son Jesus Christ as their personal Lord and Savior. Accepting God's one and only son begins with a simple prayer:

Lord Jesus, I am sorry for my sins, I am powerless to save myself, I invite you to come into my life and take charge of my life and save me. Thank you for dying on the cross for me.

If you have said that simple prayer, you are now a part of God's family. If you are not already a part of a Bible-based church, it is recommended that you visit and later join a Bible-based church to fellowship with other like-minded Christians. This also helps develop your growing relationship with God, and it gives you a support network of others that you can socialize with and count on for care, love, acceptance and support. In addition, it will give you the opportunity to discuss your finances with others who have been in the same situation as you; they can share with you how they survived it with God's help. God also wants each and every person that He created on earth to have His highest and best for their lives. Many people want God's highest and best for their lives, but they do not really want a relationship with God. You cannot have one without the other. People try and trick God into believing that they have changed, they have repented or that their hearts and motives are pure. God's response to that can be found in Jeremiah 17:10: "I the LORD search the heart and examine the mind, to reward a man according to his conduct, according to what his deeds deserve."

So a fake change or a fake repentance with God will not work in getting you a financial bailout. Money and fame may buy people, it may buy many things, and it might buy space, but it cannot buy the true hearts of men and women, it cannot buy God, and it stores up nothing of eternal value.

God wants you to display the fruits of the spirit, Galatians 5:22. The fruits of the spirit are:

1. Love
2. Joy
3. Peace
4. Longsuffering
5. Kindness
6. Goodness
7. Faithfulness
8. Gentleness
9. Self-control

If you are not displaying the fruits of the spirit, and God is not pleased with you, that may be a big factor in what has caused your financial resources to dry up. The drying up of your resources is one of the methods that God uses to chasten you when your behavior is unacceptable to His standards. God does this because He is a Holy and redemptive God, and He wants to bring about redemptive confrontation. God does not want to destroy you; He wants to change you. If you were laid off or fired and cannot find a job, you are in God's holding cell. If you are the person that makes the decision to lay people off and you are having financial difficulties, you are in God's holding cell.

If you are newly out of school, or just trying to find a new career and cannot find a job, you are in God's holding cell. The doors of your financial cell will not open until you repent of your current ways and submit to the changes God wants to make in you and in your life. If you are insistent upon the current path you are on instead of repenting and making the necessary changes God is asking you to make, your sentence in God's holding cell will continue indefinitely. There are several other factors that could contribute to your sentence in God's holding cell:

1. Are you giving God the first ten percent of your income? Leviticus 27:30: "A tithe of everything from the land, whether grain from the soil or fruit from the trees, belongs to the LORD; it is holy to the LORD."

2. Are you serving the Lord by either volunteering in a local church, a local ministry or by helping those less fortunate to come to know Jesus Christ as their personal lord and savior? Matthew 28:19: "Therefore go and make disciples of all nations, baptizing them in the name of the Father and of the Son and of the Holy Spirit."

3. Are you living beyond the amount of money you have coming in? Ecclesiastes 5:10: "Whoever loves money never has money enough; whoever loves wealth is never satisfied with his income. This too is meaningless."

4. Are you making a wise plan on how to spend the remanding ninety percent of the income you have? Make a budget, make a plan and then stick with it. Many people spend money foolishly or get paid and their whole check is gone before the end of the day. Need help? Seek out counseling to overcome this type of dysfunction.

5. Are you a good steward of the twenty-four hours that God gives you each day?

God empowered you to be a manager. Each day He gives you twenty-four hours in which He expects you to manage your time wisely. Many people give their time away by watching TV, laying around, or just sleeping all day.

Chapter 4

Why Does God Want To Give You A Financial Bailout?

God's purposes are always redemptive, irrespective as to what
methods He chooses to bring about His purposes, including
financial ruin, devastation, disappointment, setbacks, loss, or
declining economic circumstances. Although God is good, holy and
righteous, if you find yourself identifying with any of the
aforementioned categories of people, God's holy redemptive nature
influences Him to permit whatever circumstances He deems
necessary to bring about redemptive confrontation. Although God
understands your pain and your suffering as well as your anxiety
about your current situation, He has allowed no more than what
was necessary to bring you to this point in your life to get your
attention and to get you to repent of your current ways. God does
not enjoy seeing the world in its current state. Greed has replaced
love, competition and envy have replaced brotherly love, and peace
has been replaced with hate, hostility and killing.

People are being replaced by computers, corporate takeovers,
and international call centers. God looks at the world He created
and is very sad that His creatures whom He formed in His image
are choosing to behave in this manner. In Genesis 6:5-8, the Lord
saw how great man's wickedness on the earth had become, and that

every inclination of the thoughts of His heart were only evil. The Lord was grieved that He had made man on the earth, and His heart was filled with pain. So the LORD said, "I will wipe mankind, whom I have created, from the face of the earth – men and animals, and creatures that move along the ground, and birds of the air – for I am grieved that I have made them." But Noah found favor in the eyes of the LORD.

The Lord instructed Noah to build an ark because God decided to put an end to all people because the earth was filled with violence because of them. The Lord gave Noah specific instructions on how to build the ark and what to place on the ark. Noah faithfully followed God's instructions. Noah had to wait some time before God decided to send the flood, but when God did, it destroyed all of mankind. Noah and everyone on his ark were saved. God is looking around the earth and He is seeing what He saw when He sent the flood before to destroy the land. But because God is redemptive by nature, He does not want to repeat His previous act of destroying an entire world, He desires first to save you and to save the world.

God wants to give you a financial bailout plan. If you are stubborn, if you resist, if you do not believe or do not want to submit to God's way of doing things, your situation will undoubtedly worsen. God will not relent in His pursuit of you; He will continue to bring about redemptive confrontation until you are willing and ready to address and deal with the root causes of your situation. The longer you deny or pretend that you do not have any root causes, the longer you will stay in God's holding cell. The longer you make excuses for behavior that God finds offensive, inappropriate, or unacceptable, the longer you will stay in God's holding cell. Are you beginning to get the picture? God wants to give you a financial bailout, but how quickly you will receive your financial bailout depends upon you and your getting right with God. If you do what God is asking you to do in this book, you will witness God's conditional restoration of your life.

Chapter 5

What If You Don't Get The Results You Want?

Seeking God for your financial bailout is a God-given concept. When God gives a concept, an idea, a plan, or an instruction, it is His responsibility to provide the desired outcome you are seeking, not the author of this book. Numbers 23:19: "God is not a man, that he should lie, nor a son of man, that he should change his mind. Does he speak and then not act? Does he promise and not fulfill?"

Understand also that your idea of a financial bailout and God's idea of a financial bailout might be different. This may be why you might think that God's financial bailout plan does not work. Proverbs 16:9: "In his heart a man plans his course, but the LORD determines his steps."

Because your current circumstances did not come about overnight, chances are they will not be resolved overnight. True change and true repentance takes time, and so will God's financial bailout plan for your life. While you are probably just interested in obtaining your financial bailout from God, He is interested in the following for you:

1. Peace – that you may live in peace and harmony with yourself, your family, your coworkers and with God. The peace of God surpasses all understanding, Philippians 4:7.

2. Harmony – that you may learn to get along with others, help others and contribute to others. God created this world because He wanted a family. God built you for relationships. God desires you to have true and authentic relationships where old rifts, old trespasses, old grudges, and old envy as well as jealousy are dissipated. "If you do not forgive others, your father in Heaven will not forgive you." Matthew 6:15.

3. Joy – God wants you to experience joy again. Real joy comes from God. Only God or Jesus can fill your cup. People will hurt you, disappoint you, and they will leave you. True joy comes from God, and God will never leave you. "The joy of the Lord will become your strength." Nehemiah 8:10.

4. Kingdom work – God wants you to be interested in Him and His kingdom. Many people only want God to fulfill their interests, but God wants you to be interested in Him. Many people only call upon God when they are in trouble, or when they want or need something. This is not an authentic spirit-filled life. God wants you to spend time reading the Bible, spend time praying, spend time going to church, spend time worshiping Him in a Bible-based church. God wants you to introduce others to Him that do not know Him.

5. Reach back – God wants you to have a sincere desire to help those that are less fortunate. In today's society we have the haves and the have not's. Many of the people who have put on a huge front as if they really help people when they really do not. What they do is help those within their circle or within the confines of organizations and or groups they like. The rest, no matter how good their cause or how worthy their cause, get left behind. In most cases those that have amassed wealth are not really interested in reaching back and

helping the unknown person, the undiscovered person, or the person of little means. There are, however, a limited number of people who have wealth that do help those less fortunate that are not in their click, but it is not enough. The poor, the needy, and the destitute realize this, and this is what makes them angry, bitter, and it is what influences them to turn to a life of crime. This is one of the reasons why wealthy people are targets for theft and kidnapping. Although no one is totally responsible for the ones who have not, God blesses those who have wealth to be a blessing to others. God doesn't say bless the ones you like and then ignore the others. Genesis 12:1-3 speaks of how God's plans of blessing should work:

"The LORD had said to Abram, 'Leave your country, your people and your father's household and go to the land I will show you. I will make you into a great nation and I will bless you; I will make your name great, and you will be a blessing. I will bless those who bless you, and whoever curses you I will curse; and all peoples on earth will be blessed through you."

God's plan was to bless the nation of Israel, so it in turn could bless other nations.

Chapter 6

Prayer's Power To Usher In Your God-Given Financial Bailout

"Be anxious for nothing, but in everything by prayer and supplication with thanksgiving, make your requests known to God." Philippians 4:6. Prayer is communication with God. You speak to God, and God listens. God answers your prayers, often in ways that many people do not recognize. God also answers prayers in His own time and in His own way. Many do not understand this and are left frustrated, angry and bitter because they feel that either God does not hear them, God does not answer, or their request will not be granted. An example of how God answers prayer is this book. I had no intention of writing this book due to my hectic schedule. God spoke to me and told me of the many cries for His help He is receiving through prayer. I in turn accepted His request to pen this book for Him so the help that many need could be obtained.

As a result, my own agenda was changed, my schedule was interrupted, my plans were put on hold, and my life would never be the same all because someone had prayed. When you pray, you never know who God will work through to bring about the answers to your prayers. God does answer prayer, although He may not answer your prayer in the specific time you want, the specific way you want, or He may not give you the specific outcome that you are looking for. You currently live in the earthly realm, or the physical realm. God is a spirit and although God's presence is in the earth, God prefers to work in the spiritual realm. Since only God has the power to change what you need changed, you have to meet Him on His 'turf' in the spiritual realm. The way you meet God in the spiritual realm is through your prayers and your supplications. When you pray, you enter into God's realm – the spiritual realm. Your requests, your feelings, and your fears are then placed in God's hands. God then answers your prayers in the spirit realm, but the answers are manifested in the earth or physical realm, which is where you are. The prayers are answered through God's spirit, which are people. When you make your prayer petitions known, God answers through the spirit of the people He created, and since I am one of those people, He is answering through me because the spirit of God lives in me. Prayer is a very powerful tool that will bring amazing results.

Prayer changes things, prayer changes people, prayer changes times, and prayer changes outcomes. To not pray is a costly mistake you cannot afford to make, even more so in your current circumstances.

The following short prayers are recommended to get you started until you establish your own dialogue with God.

Prayer for Restoration

Creator of the Heavens and the earth, send revival, send restoration, restore back to me the years that the swarming locust, the cankerworm, the caterpillar, and the palmerworm have eaten up or taken from me, Joel 2:25. Help me to change into the type of person that honors you and honors others, bringing you glory. Forgive me of my shortcomings and remember not the sins of my youth. Let me cast my net on the right side of the boat as did the disciples when they were following Jesus, let me find plenty to fill my needs, John 21:6. In Jesus' name I ask and pray. Amen.

Prayer for Forgiveness

Great is my sin before You; I hide my face from You because of my wicked and evil ways. Cleanse me from all unrighteousness and draw me into a deeper relationship with You. Let me sit at Your feet until I learn what it is that You want me to know, and how it is that You want me to be. Forgive me for my many transgressions, my evil deeds, my evil thoughts, and my wrong focus. Hide me in the secret place that You speak of in Psalm 91. Great are my burdens, deep is my grief, dark and slippery is my path. Shine your light of hope into my life and rescue me from the bottom of the pit that I find myself in. Praise be to You, Father of lights, for hearing me and for having mercy upon me and my soul. Amen.

Prayer for Guidance

Lord, I am lost. In my pathway is nothing but brokenness, disappointment, failure, and gloom. In the hustle and bustle of this world, I have conformed to the world's way of doing things, achieving things, and wanting things. I have lusted for worldly things, worldly places, and worldly people. Realizing now that only those things that are eternal will matter, I ask for Your help, dear God, in guiding me back into a right relationship with You, a right focus with You, restore me and my finances so that I may once again live at peace with You, live at peace with myself and live at peace with all mankind. Lead me to a better pathway, a pathway that will be filled with love, Your presence, and Your goodness. Develop in me the nine fruits of the spirit that You speak of in Your Holy Word so that I can be kind, gentle and loving in all of my ways. Amen.

Prayer to Know Jesus

Jesus, I want to know You. Jesus I want to fellowship with You, I want to understand the time that You spent here on earth. Teach me how to live in a way that will not only please You but will please God and the Holy Spirit as well. Teach me what You learned from God that helped You so immensely to live such a pure and sinless life.

Give me the secrets of resting in God's presence. Share with me the ancient secrets that kept You from giving in to the world's temptations, the world's traps, and the world's systems. Empower me to make good financial decisions so that they are in line with God's will, God's plans and God's purposes for my life. Empower me with cutting-age strategies to overcome the wiles of the devil, who is constantly attacking my life, my finances, my hope, and my future in hopes of bringing me to financial ruin. Show me the abundant life You spoke of in John 10:10 when You said that You had come to give life and to give it more abundantly! Amen.

Prayer for Pardon

Pardon me, dear God, not because I deserve it but because You deserve it. You sent Your one and only son into this world to die for me more than 2,000 years ago and He paid a huge price for my sins. It is a debt that I can never repay because of Jesus' sacrifice for me and because of Your sacrifice for me I am sorry for my sins. I am ashamed of how I have been. I am ashamed of the decisions that I have made and the pathways that I have taken. I hunger for Your restoration, Your forgiveness and Your mercy. Pardon me, dear God, and help me become all that You created me to be. In Jesus' name I ask and pray. Amen.

Prayer for Protection as you Seek God for a Financial Bailout

God, there are many that chase after me. From dawn to dusk they give me no peace, they give me no kindness, no mercy and no grace. You have seen this, You have heard this. Do not hide Your face from me, dear God, and do not relent from launching forward Your power in my situation to help me. Dear God, do not let my enemies and creditors overtake me. By my own hands I have allowed the creditors to place a noose around my neck, they are drawing the noose tighter and tighter and tighter. Lord, I am gasping for air, I am gasping for breath, I am going down low, save me as only You can. Swoop down low and intervene and rescue my life from the multitudes of those who chase after me. Help me get out of this tangled up net that I have created for myself. Be my shield and buckler against the fiery darts of the enemy as they seek to take my peace, seek to take my mind, and seek to take away all that I have and all that I own. Rescue my life from the clutches of those who chase after me. God, You have seen their unfair practices and their unfair acts, at just the right time, dear God, act and give me a financial bailout as only You can. Amen.

Chapter 7

For Leaders Seeking A Financial Bailout From God

Leaders are given a special charge from God to lead, whether they realize it or not. As a leader, you are placed in a position of authority to oversee projects, to oversee people, and to oversee situations. As a leader, you have certain powers, certain responsibilities, and certain rights. God holds leaders to a higher standard because, as a leader, you are entrusted with more, and you are given the position with the expectation that you will make fair and just decisions. You are expected to be a Godly role model so those that come after you will have a pattern of excellence to follow. You are entrusted with people's lives with the expectation that you will be kind, caring and compassionate towards those that are either sent your way or brought your way. This is the type of leader that loves and honors God with their leadership position.

If you are experiencing pain as a leader, there is a reason for it. Most leaders think that there is nothing wrong with their leadership style. Most leaders have a high opinion of themselves, and the leadership style that they follow. This is what has caused the current problems. It is their own opinion of themselves that they have based their decisions upon, and it is their own opinions that keep them from changing. It is their own opinions that keep them from hearing what God is trying to say to them. God, however, in most cases has another opinion of the leader, and this is why the leader finds him/herself in their current financial predicament. Here are some additional reasons why God may put leaders in His holding cell:

1. God has not been able to get the leader's attention so the leader can clearly understand what God's message is.
2. God is trying to change the leader's direction, but the leader is not getting the message or is resisting the message and God's methods.
3. God wants the leader's presentation style to change.
4. God wants the leader's outreach strategy to change.
5. God is dealing with the leader because of mismanaged finances, frivolous spending, and/or a misplaced focus.

If you are a leader in ministry, God chooses leaders for Him and for His people because of the condition of their hearts. Man looks at the outward appearance, but the Lord looks at the heart, 1 Samuel 16:7. Consider David in 1 Samuel 16:12. David was a loner, a shepherd boy; he wasn't even voted to be picked by God by his own father. David really loved the Lord, he walked with God, he talked with God, and he sang songs to God. This pleased the heart of God. The problem with ministry is the long hours, the huge time demands, the excessively long services, the demands and neediness of the people, and the constant struggle to increase donations and increase attendance. It is often difficult to stay sane, balanced and grounded in the Word of God when the pressures, stresses and demands are so high. God understands pastoral and ministry "burnouts" and offers to help. Psalm 55:22 says: "Cast your cares on the LORD and he will sustain you; he will never let the righteous fall."

Many ministry leaders preach and teach the message of resting in the Lord, but many do not heed their own advice, and this is what causes the ministerial burnout and the secret desire to escape

the ministry. Somewhere along the ministerial journey hearts
change, and the change is justified as "growing apart", or
differences. A spirit-filled Christian that loves God does not grow
apart from God, or grow apart from the ministry, or from the mate
that God has given them. What happens is that the spirit-filled
Christian grows apart from the demands of the ministry, the stresses
of the ministry, the demands and the neediness of the people and
the excessively long hours. Because the leader is not thinking clearly,
and because of the excessive demands, they think they have grown
apart from the ministry or from God or their mate.

When you are a well-balanced leader, and you have learned to
place your schedule in perspective in regards to your time, your
service, and your strategic outreaches for attendance and donations,
you are happy, your relationship with God blossoms and flourishes,
and your finances are strong and you have plenty left over to
contribute to those less fortunate than yourself. You have learned to
put God first, your spouse second, your family third, and everything
else is categorized according to its fit in your life. Your relationship
with God, if you are in a right relationship with Him, should cause
an acceleration of your destiny rather than a foreclosure. Your
destiny is stalled, hindered, and cut short when you are not in a right
relationship with God. If you are not in a right relationship with
God and you are a leader, God's Holy nature obligates Him to bring
about whatever He deems necessary to cause redemptive
confrontation.

If the leader resists God's methods and God's process to
change them, God may use more drastic measures to accomplish
His purposes. If you are a leader seeking a financial bailout from
God, your financial bailout may take longer to manifest because of
the magnitude of responsibility that you have been given, and
because of any damage you may have inflicted upon others. God
does forgive, but He does not always remove the consequence that
may have developed as a result of inappropriate behavior
immediately. A good analogy to compare God's financial bailout
process to is the healing of a broken bone. When a bone is broken
in your leg, you know it. It hurts and it becomes painful to walk.

Usually the person experiencing the broken bone is either rushed to the hospital or taken to the doctor. The doctor usually orders an x-ray, and when he receives the x-ray, he makes a determination of how best to proceed with the broken bone. Typically, the doctor orders a cast to be placed on the bone. The cast remains on the person's leg for an indefinite period of time depending upon how well and how quickly the leg heals. You may have to use crutches to get around for the time period that your leg is in a cast. During your stay with the doctor, he may order certain tests and make other recommendations depending upon your specific situation to help facilitate your healing process. In order to heal, it is imperative for you to follow the doctor's instructions, use the support tools that he recommends, take any medicine that he gives you to relieve pain, and get plenty of rest and relaxation. If you follow your doctor's instructions, your bones will heal within a specific time frame. Seeking God for your financial bailout process is no different.

When you begin to seriously seek God for your financial bailout, He will examine you right where you are, He will examine your finances, and He will examine the condition of your heart. He has already observed what kind of character, what kind of integrity, and what kind of temperament you have. Once you become serious, you begin to experience the cast God has on you because God begins to work on your situation while you are in His holding cell. From time to time, God will order certain tests and certain additional requirements to determine where you are in His process. Depending upon what the test results reveal, you either get to go forward towards receiving your financial bailout plan, or you remain in God's holding cell. If you have truly changed and truly repented in time, you will receive the financial bailout plan you need and want to be able to experience God's total restoration in your life. Because most people just want God's financial bailout plan for their life, and they do not really want a relationship with God, they will never make it out of God's holding cell and will continue to experience one financial disappointment after another. If you pretend long enough to receive a financial bailout plan from God, and your change and or repentance is not real, you will quickly realize, what happens when a person tries to mock God. Do not be deceived, God cannot be mocked. A man reaps what he sows, Galatians 6:7.

All healing comes from God. So your financial bailout is like the healing of a broken leg, although God has the power to heal instantly, He very rarely does this. He prefers to heal over time to give the body, mind, and spirit time to heal, and to work out the changes He desires to make in the lives of those looking to be healed. God prefers a total healing rather than just to heal the body and not the mind and the spirit. To just heal the body will still result in illness which could cause additional problems down the line. As a leader, people's lives depends upon the decisions that you make, so it is imperative that you make decisions with a clear mind, from a right relationship with God, and with the best interest of that person in mind. Overworked, angry and bitter leaders do not make good decisions for anyone, including themselves. It is imperative that you get right with God so that you can either get to keep your leadership position or resume your leadership position.

If you are a leader and you are right with God, but you are still experiencing financial loss, financial setbacks, and no financial provisions from God, you may be experiencing the dark valley of the financial strain so that you can better identify with the suffering of the people that God has called you to lead. That was the reason Jesus had to live on this earth as a human being, so He would be able to identify with the sufferings, the betrayals, and the ups and downs of life. "To this you were called because Christ suffered for you, leaving you an example that you should follow. He committed no sin, and no deceit was found in his mouth. When they hurled their insults at Him, He did not retaliate; when He suffered, He made no threats. Instead, He entrusted himself to Him who judges justly", 1 Peter 2:21-24. If you feel that you are right with God, and if after reading this book God has not shown you anything different, then God has you right where you are so you can get firsthand knowledge of what His people are going through. An effective leader or an effective minister cannot adequately address and minister to the pain of His people until they have firsthand knowledge of their experiences and pain through suffering themselves.

As a leader, people want you to understand how they feel, people want you to see how they feel, people want you to be able to relate to how they feel. People want you to have like-minded experiences to share with them so they can know and understand how God worked in your life. This inspires them and gives them more hope than a prewritten sermon, or a tape or DVD. People want to know that you are human, and that you worry. People want to know that you too have sleepless nights. People want to know that you look for God in the same ways that they do. People need to know that God doesn't always answer your prayers in the way that you want, or in the time that you want. People want to know that it is okay to be scared and to have serious fears, and serious fears that just don't seem to go away no matter how much and how hard you pray. This is why your struggle to get out of your current circumstances may not end prematurely or may take a long time. God has you in a process that is necessary to strengthen you, educate you and make you more fruitful for His kingdom.

Chapter 8

Rebuilding Your Life After God Gives You Your Financial Bailout

If you have faithfully followed the directions given in this book, you should start to see gradual improvement in not only your life but in your finances and your outlook on life. In addition, the peace and real happiness you previously lacked should slowly but surely start to be restored. With revelation knowledge being given to you, you are now responsible for keeping this knowledge close and never deviating from the right pathway of God's righteousness. One of the greatest joys to God's heart is when one sinner repents, mends his ways, has a change of heart and becomes a pleasant and contributing citizen rather than a source of conflict and pain that causes others to experience misfortune, doom and failure. "I tell you that there will be more rejoicing in Heaven over one sinner who repents than over ninety-nine righteous people who do not need to repent," Luke 15:7.

As your life begins to change and you begin to see the long overdue breakthrough you wanted and needed, it is important to not make rash decisions without first considering all the facts and without looking at your entire financial situation. One of the reasons many people are placed in God's holding cell is because of a mismanagement of credit cards, and because of living outside the income God has supplied them with. If God has brought you out from this type of situation, it is imperative you understand that unless you gain control of your spending habits, you will wind right back up in the same situation again. If you are guilty of charging and paying later, have you really considered the cost of using credit?

Using credit can be costly. Interest rates can be extremely high and making the minimum payment oftentimes does little to reduce the balance. For example if you borrow $2,000.00 and you make the minimum monthly payment each month, that single charge could wind up costing you close to $7,000.00. Other excessive charges on credit cards include "over the limit" charges, late charges, and cash advance charges. These extra charges add to your daily balance along with interest charges that may apply. It is wise to ask yourself before making purchases whether you really need the item (or do you just want the item?). If you just want the item, it would be wise not to purchase the item on credit. If you really need the item, it would be wise to attempt first to save the money necessary to buy the item with cash. If the item is a big ticket item, it would be wise to shop around for the best price and the best credit card provider with the best interest rate prior to making the purchase.

God withholds certain blessings and benefits from you if He sees that you cannot manage your finances and handle credit wisely! Here are two websites to help you learn more about credit and how to manage your credit:

1. www.crown.org or crown financial 1-800-722-1976
2. www.daveramsey.com or Dave Ramsey 1-888-227-3223

The goal here is to learn the right way to handle your finances and credit, so you do not have to fall back into the situation you currently find yourself in. Seeking professional help is not a sign of weakness but a sign of strength; so do not be afraid to seek out help from those more knowledgeable than you. Those on your same level cannot adequately instruct you because they have no clue how to get out of their own situations, or they would have already.

Another important factor to consider if God has given you your financial bailout is creating a budget. Although you may not have much money coming in, or your expenses may far exceed your income, it is still very wise to create a budget. Many people feel so overwhelmed and distraught by their situation that they fail to make a plan, and therefore through default they mismanage the money that they do have coming in. The money they have is usually spent on the basic necessities, and everything else gets either put on hold, ignored, or not paid. Collectors' phone calls are ignored and collections letters are either stacked up in a pile or totally discarded. A budget is a written plan that creates a snapshot of what is going on with your finances. Without a snapshot of what is going on or without a record of how you are spending your money, you may lose track of where you are spending money, or not see ways that you could reduce the amount of money you are spending. As difficult as it is to be rational at this point, you somehow have to find the will to go on, and the desire to wisely plan how to manage what you have coming in. "Plans fail for lack of counsel, but with many advisors they succeed", Proverbs 15:22.

If you still find it difficult to deal with your own finances or create a budget, the following website should help you:

http://www.practicalmoneyskills.com/english/index.php
- Click on 'at home'
- Look under 'learning centers'
- Click on 'budgeting'

The website will give you detailed information on how to create a budget, how to use a budget, and how to benefit from a budget. For those who do not have Internet access, the company can be reached at the following contact information:

1-800-Visa-511 or write to:
Practical Money Skills for Life
Attn: Corporate Relations.
P.O. Box 194607 San Francisco, CA 94119-4607

It is imperative that when God gives you a financial bailout you do not forget Him – the giver of all that you have. "Now they know that everything you have given me comes from you," John 17:7.

Remember, God expects you to give Him the first ten percent of all your income. You might think that you already do not have enough money. But although this may be true, God will honor you with more if you honor Him with the first ten percent of your income. This is the law of sowing and reaping. Every time you give God ten percent of your income, you are sowing a seed into His kingdom's work. God promises that for everyone that sows seeds, in return you will receive a harvest. Your harvest is always much larger than the seed you have sown. Have you ever noticed how farmers buy huge quantities of seeds and plant them at the right time? When the seed comes to the age of maturity, the seed returns a harvest. A great example is the planting of a watermelon seed. The seed is very tiny. The farmer plants the seed, he then waters it, and then God makes it grow and returns back to the farmer a harvest, which is a big juicy ripe watermelon.

People who are not sowing the first ten percent of their income experience the same thing that would happen if you walked up to a bank and put in your ATM card without having any money in the bank. You go to the bank with an expectation of being able to withdraw large amounts of money, but the machine just gives you an error message telling you that you have insufficient funds to complete this transaction; it may even take your card because you have attempted to withdraw money when you have nothing in the bank. Sowing seeds into God's work will always return an even bigger harvest from God. Your harvest is determined by God and is usually orchestrated by His own timing and in His own way. It is the accumulation of your seeds that will determine the harvest in your due season. "Do not grow weary in well doing, You will reap a harvest in due season if you faint not," Galatians 6:9.

"As long as the earth endures, seedtime and harvest, cold and heat, summer and winter, day and night will never cease", Genesis 8:22. Never underestimate the power of sowing seeds into God's Kingdom by sowing the first ten percent of your income. Consequently, when people that are not right with God, or people who do not come to full repentance before God, do not make the changes God is asking them to make before Him, the planting of seeds by sowing into God's Kingdom does not work. It does not work because God's blessings are often conditional, and if God has placed you in His holding cell because of your current behavior, your current mismanagement of funds, or because of other reasons that He will reveal to you, He will not elevate you to another level of financial responsibility until you come in line with His request for change in your life as outlined in this book. You can't buy God with money, with acts of service, with empty promises or with your popularity, God is looking at the condition of your heart, and He is looking at His standards and comparing where you are now as opposed to where you should be. If He fails to move you closer to where you should be by just gentle nudging and gentle instruction, you are placed in God's holding cell until further notice. Sowing seeds through tithing will not change your outcome when what God wants to change is *you*.

When God gives you your financial bailout, it is imperative that after you create your budget you think long-term and start planning to save money. As you slowly get back on your feet and the storm begins to subside, long-range planning is critical to your success. Many people work for years with no thought for tomorrow and then find out that social security is not enough to meet their needs, food stamps are not enough to meet their needs, and government aid is not enough either. Connecting with financial planners who specialize in retirement plans, saving bonds, and high-yield stocks is highly recommended.

Recommended resources for retirement planning are listed below:

http://www.guidestonefunds.org/
http://www.mma online.org

When your finances stabilize, contact one or both of the above firms, or any firm of your choice, and ask for their help in arranging your long-term retirement plan, you will be glad you did.

Chapter 9

Thanking God For The Financial Bailout He Has Given You

How many times have you done something for someone, gone out of your way for someone, or gone above and beyond the call of duty for someone and they never glanced your way and said, "Thank you."

The words "thank you" are two very small and easy words to say, but why do most people either lack the common courtesy to say them or not realize that although God is a spirit He has feelings, thoughts, and also desires to be thanked for the things He has done in and through your life? Jesus experienced in Luke 17:11-19 ungrateful lepers that did not say "thank you".

While Jesus was on His way to Jerusalem, He was passing through Samira and Galilee. As He entered the village He encountered ten leprous men. They stood at a distance from Him and raised their voices saying, "Jesus have mercy upon us." Jesus saw them and told them to go show themselves to the priest, and as they were going they were cleansed. Only one of them, after seeing that he had been healed, turned back with a loud shout and glorified God before falling on his face at Jesus' feet, giving thanks to Him. And he was a Samaritan. Then Jesus answered and said, "Were there not ten cleansed? But the nine – where are they? Was no one found who returned to give glory to God except this foreigner?" And He said to him, "Stand up and go; your faith has made you well." Jesus healed ten lepers, but only one was grateful enough to turn back and say "thank you" to God.

Although you may have never thought about thanking God for all that He has done and all that He continues to do in your life, it is never too late to start. If you have always thanked God for what He has done in your life and for what He continues to do in your life, take it a step further. Deepen your intimacy with God, remove the grammatically correct stances and get real with God – tell Him how you really feel.

To totally experience God's bailout plan, as well as heal in mind and spirit, you have to be willing to release all of the hurt, all of the pain, and all of the anger and bitterness that you harbored towards God while you were in His holding cell. You have to come clean with yourself and come clean with God so that you can experience total healing.

Take a journal or pad and select a place where you can be alone with God undisturbed for at least an hour each day for seven days. Now write down all of your feelings about what happened to you, why you thought what happened to you occurred, and how you felt about what God allowed to happen to you. Clearly indicate in your journal or on your pad how this book helped you to come to a greater understanding of who you are and what part you played in being in God's holding cell. Determine what you learned about yourself while you were in God's holding cell, and what you learned about God while you were there. The number seven represents spiritual perfection in the Bible; it means divine fulness, completeness and totality. After you have completed this seven-day one-hour exercise, reread your thoughts and ideas about your experience in God's holding cell and surrender the entire pad or journal to God. Ask Him to heal you from the rage, the anger, the bitterness and the hurt that you felt. Ask God to make an exchange with you whereby you will give Him your ashes if He will give you His beauty, Isaiah 61:3. Grieve if you need to, get mad if you want to, and do whatever you need to do to get it all out of your system. But do get it all out, it is imperative that you experience God's financial bailout with an uncontaminated spirit and mind.

The greatest way to show God that you are thankful for all that He has done for you is to verbally tell Him "thank you". You can also share your story and your testimonies with others who may have been in the same situation with you. You may know others who are facing what you faced, and you may be their only hope. Shed your fear and your desire to keep your situation a secret and reach out and touch someone else facing the incredible pain that you endured. Share your discovery of this book with them; either loan the book to them or show them where they can purchase it. The book is modestly priced so that anyone who wants God's financial bailout plan will be able to access it. The book alone is not the cure, the author of this book is not the cure, God's power is the cure. To access God's power, the person will need to read the book in its entirety and make the desired changes that God requires. Because this book is a God-given concept, the purchaser's results from reading this book may vary depending upon God's plans and or purposes for their lives.

Introduce the book to your employer, your pastor, your family members, and your friends, help them learn how to help themselves so that they can experience God's financial bailout plan in their lives. "Do all this for the sake of the gospel, that you may share in its blessings," 1 Corinthians 9:23. You may be the catalyst that God decides to use to help someone else out of their miry pit of clay. Keeping your story to yourself helps only you, sharing it with others helps you and it helps others. In sharing your stories with others, you will come to realize that through your process of seeking God for your financial bailout, God has made you stronger, wiser and better. You now have a testimony to share with the world that can help people overcome their financial dilemma as well as help them to become a much better person who experiences peace, happiness, God's love, God's plans and God's purposes for their lives. As you become more open about what happened to you and how God worked in your life to bring you through, God will send you people that He wants you to help to come to this same revelation knowledge that you experienced as a result of reading this book. Some of the people will be so broken by their circumstances that they have lost the hope and the will to go on. Some of the people will have stories that far exceed anything you had to go through or anything that you have ever heard of before.

In order to prepare for the influx of people that God will send when you make yourself available and open for His use, it is highly recommended that you prepare yourself emotionally and mentally. God gave each born-again believer the indwelling Holy Spirit. Jesus said, "If you love me, you will obey what I command. And I will ask the Father, and He will give you another Counselor to be with you forever the Spirit of truth. The world cannot accept Him, because it neither sees Him nor knows Him. But you know Him, for He lives with you and will be in you. I will not leave you as orphans; I will come to you. Before long, the world will not see me anymore, but you will see me. Because I live, you also will live," John 14:15-19. "But the Counselor, the Holy Spirit, whom the Father will send in my name, will teach you all things and will remind you of everything I have said to you," John 14:26.

If you surrender to the Holy Spirit's work within you, He will help you to become the type of person who has the heart to help others. The Holy Spirit will empower you with the right words to say to those that are hurting. The Holy Spirit will give you knowledge beyond your years to advise others. The Holy Spirit will give you knowledge beyond your experience to soothe others, and knowledge beyond human reasoning to facilitate life change and life reconstruction. Wisdom will sprout forth from your mouth to enable others to experience God's healing power and God's peace as you surrender your life and your plans to God's Holy redemptive work. The Holy Spirit will teach you how to discern when you are going the right way and when you are not in terms of living your life, advising others and making financial decisions. If you submit to the Holy Spirit's work in your life, you may never have to be placed in God's holding cell again. The Holy Spirit is like a GPS (Global Positioning System); He leads you in the right direction and calls for a course correction when you are heading the wrong way. It pleases the heart of God to give the Holy Spirit to each born-again believer. God wants you to succeed, not fail, and that is why He gives you so many chances and so many resources and so much assistance to help empower you to experience His success and favor.

Chapter 10

Walking Forward With God After Your God-Given Financial Bailout

Reading this book should have opened your eyes to many different truths and revealed to you many different aspects of who you are and how God works. If you have been fortunate enough to be given a financial bailout from God, it is important to remember that just because God has given you a financial bailout, it does not mean that your relationship with Him is over. If you have done everything right, your relationship with God should have deepened, and you should be experiencing a new level of intimacy with God. You should not only feel more comfortable in your own skin, but your perspective on life and living should have changed. You should also feel comfortable with God and there should exist within you a greater level of comfort with God, His methods and His way. Once you begin to see and understand how God works in your life, you should come to a realization that although you may not understand why God does what He does, He does have your best interests at heart, and you can trust and know that His heart towards you is good. "'For I know the plans I have for you,' declares the Lord, "plans to prosper you and not to harm you, plans to give you hope and a future." Jer. 29:11 (NIV).

Walking forward with God simply means including God in your

daily plans, your daily prayers, and your daily conversations. A good habit to cultivate is to rise early in the morning and pray. Set aside a quiet time each day where you spend the first part of the day praying. To make the most of your day consider the following:

1. Ask God to protect you this day.
2. Ask God to deliver you from evil this day.
3. Ask God to order and direct your day in such a way that helps you accomplish your plans and purposes that will include His plans and purposes for your life.
4. Ask God to give you "God encounters" and God-sized dreams and plans to give Him glory and honor on the earth.
5. Ask God to help you learn more about tithing and His "sowing and reaping" principles.
6. Ask God to help you plan and manage your spending habits on a daily basis.

Walking forward with God can be a wonderful experience for you as you become comfortable following God's leads, and as you become comfortable learning more about God, His statutes, His ways, and His methods. Walking with God when experienced the right way is similar to walking with one of your parents in a beautiful garden when you were younger. When you entered the garden, you may not have known your way around, you may have enjoyed and loved the scenery. Because you were with your parent and you did not know your way around, your parent held your hand as you were shown all around the beautiful garden. As you walked around the garden, your parent may have narrated what each part of the garden meant and explained the many different variations of flowers present. This is how God holds you when you are in His holding cell and you do not know why you are there. But as a gentle and loving parent, God loves you too much to let you go on the way you were. "Thus says the Lord, Your Redeemer, the Holy One of Israel: "I am the Lord your God, who teaches you to profit, who leads you by the way you should go." (Isaiah 48:17)

Although starting your morning with God is good, it is imperative that you set aside specific time in your afternoon or evening to have a more in depth time with God and His Word the Holy Bible. The Bible has been labeled as being the "Basic Instruction Book before leaving earth book"; most of the answers to life's questions can be found in the Bible. If you are a seasoned veteran in the study of the Bible, perhaps God is calling you to learn and teach at a greater theological level of expertise. If this is so, reading the Bible could have lost its challenge to you. In order to revive a waning desire for the Bible, ask the Holy Spirit to breathe new life into you for God's Word. Ask the Holy Spirit to illuminate the Bible to you in a theological way so that the eyes and ears of your understanding will be opened, unplugged and saturated with the depth of the knowledge that God wants to impart into you. You can then go forth as a beacon shedding light in dark places and bringing hope to the hopeless.

If you are a baby Christian, someone who is new to the Bible and has no understanding of the Bible, ask the Holy Spirit to help you understand the scriptures in the Bible. Ask the Holy Spirit to give you a supreme hunger for the Word of God. Ask the Holy Spirit to lead you to the right church and to plant you firmly in a small Bible study group designed to teach you more about God and His ways. If you have no interest in the Bible or God and His ways, you should seriously consider why you want a financial bailout from God when you are not interested in a relationship with God. God will undoubtedly sustain you in this life, but you will always be operating at less than your full capacity, and you will always receive less than God's highest and best. To change that, you have to become willing to change, you have to become willing to be open to God, and you have to become willing to have an authentic relationship with God.

Walking forward with God can be more delightful each day as God begins to give you a new appreciation of who He is and who He created you to be. Simply basking in His presence as you go about your daily tasks and your daily chores will be easier as you begin to understand that God created you with a plan in mind for your life and for a purpose that He predetermined. As you begin to experience more and more of God's financial bailout plan for your life, ask God to show you your purpose in life. Sure, having things, and acquiring wealth is good, but that is not what it is all about. Only those things that are eternal will stand. This world is only a brief journey compared to where you will spend eternity. "It is beautiful how God has done everything at the right time. He has put a sense of eternity in people's minds. Yet, mortals still can't grasp what God is doing from the beginning to the end of time," Ecclesiastes 3:11. You came into this world with nothing, and when you leave this earth you will leave with nothing. If you are fortunate enough to have accepted Jesus Christ as your personal Lord and Savior, after your departure from earth you will be lucky enough to spend all of eternity with God.

Many people have attempted to describe eternity, but the evidence of the actual eternity that will be experienced remains hidden by God. It is not to say that God cannot reveal eternity to any and everyone, God simply chooses not to. There have been reported cases of people claiming to die and go to Heaven or slip into eternity, although that may be so, eternity still remains a mystery to most. Speculators believe that eternity will be much too beautiful and wonderful to fathom here while on earth. Consequently, some things are better left unsaid and some places are better left unshown until the right time. As time goes on, you will begin to enjoy walking forward with God, you will learn more and more about God each and every day. Although no one knows for sure why God does what He does at all times, it has often been said that God works in mysterious ways. One of the ways that God might want to work is through you as one of His mysterious ways.

While you are on your journey with God remember the small things, and remember the following:

1. Reach back for those who are less fortunate than you.
2. Be kind to others.
3. Place people over profits in companies.
4. Live in the present in all situations.

5. Be authentic with yourself and others (drop the mask).
6. Retailers—change how you handle your sales and "Black Friday".
7. Appreciate and value the elderly, treat them with dignity, respect, care, and consideration.
8. Punish the guilty, remove the guilty. Reward the innocent and let the innocent go free.
9. "Flee sexual immorality,"(1 Corinthians 6:18). That is, do not have sex with someone who is not your spouse. Obedience requires that sex be reserved for one's spouse.
10. Drug dealers—get a job instead of contributing to a mind-altering dependency that causes psychological conditions and drug-induced crimes.
11. Companies—give customers what they pay for instead of seeking large payments and then providing little or no service.
12. Politicians—tell the people what you will do and do it instead of telling them what they want to hear and then breaking your promises.
13. Insurance companies—pay claims when they are due. Lawmakers, enact laws and rules to ensure this instead of allowing non-payment when payments are rightfully due.
14. Hospitals, schools, Banks, retailers, etc.—hire more staff members. Your profit margin is not more important than your service to customers. If you increased your service to customers, your profits would take care of themselves.

About the Author

Wendy Evans is an anointed evangelist, motivational speaker, writer and teacher. Gifted by God, she is the founder of WIN International Ministries.

Thank you for spending time reading and applying the God-given concepts of *Seeking God For Your Financial Bailout*. If you have successfully applied the God-given concepts in this book, then you should be experiencing your financial bailout from God.

I pray that God's highest and best will continue to be yours as you learn to seek Him first! Look for more books to come as the spirit of the Lord directs, rearranges, and intervenes! God bless!

Visit us on the web at: www.wendyevans.org

www.ingramcontent.com/pod-product-compliance
Lightning Source LLC
Chambersburg PA
CBHW031528040426
42445CB00009B/449